How to Pack

for a

World Cruise

Jackie Chase

www.adventuretravelpress.com

How to Pack for a World Cruise
By Jackie Chase

www.adventuretravelpress.com, Lady Lake, FL 32159
Copyright © 2018 by Jackie Chase

Ordering Information: Quantity sales. Special discounts are available on quantity purchases by corporations, associations, and others. For details, contact the "Special Sales Department" at the E-mail address above.

How to Pack for a World Cruise
By Jackie Chase
Print: *ISBN-978-1-937630-23-2*
E-book: *ISBN- 978-1-937630-24-9*
www.JackieChase.com; www.CulturesOfTheWorld.com

Interviews. | Tourism

Foreword

There is no better teacher than experience. There has been a need for this book so that every long-cruise guest can learn from someone who has been there and has observed issues and can recommend many valuable tips on "How To" prepare.

How to Pack for a World Cruise   by Jackie Chase

✦ Introduction

This book is meant to be your personal guide for the basics needed for a world cruise or any segment of one. Adjust according to all conditions that match your individual taste and cruise, such as a shorter segment which is part of a longer cruise itinerary. The packing numbers are based on a 120-day trip. If you use this guide for either male or female, and do not use ground vehicles to reach the embarkation port, you may try to limit yourself to one checked bag, one carry-on with wheels, [a standard 22/15/9 size], and one backpack for under the seat. You can carry the backpack on top of the wheeled luggage walking to the gate and through security so there are no heavy bags to deal with after checking the heavy 50lb one at the counter. The weight and size of what you pack is up to you, but this book will help every reader to save time, money, and frustration as they prepare for a memorable cruise, well beyond the typical one week at sea.

Please email me any comments, concerns or questions, no matter how simple they might sound. Put in the subject line the word "cruise" and send to jakartamoon@hotmail.com

<u>Bon Voyage!</u>

Chapter 1: Actions before the Cruise Begins

There are many considerations when packing; starting early is a huge advantage for organizing. Keep a notebook in case an idea comes up about what to take or do before leaving.

Consider several columns or sections. One list can be for to-dos before leaving, one for what to pack for the trip, one for what to buy for the trip, and one for ideas about projects to work on during the trip, or titles of books to rent, borrow, or buy for the trip.

Keep a list of questions to ask the cruise line or travel agent. Keep in mind that the cruise-line agent may not have all the answers. They may not have cruised on the ship you are booking or conditions may have changed. What an agent tells you may be incorrect.

For example, there was a photo of a sofa/couch on the ship's website for the room I wanted to book, and I asked the representative if that meant there was a sofa in that category of room and she said yes, of course it does. When I embarked, I asked the reception desk why my room didn't have a sofa and they advised that those photos are only suggested ideas of what might be in your room. I asked how one would know for sure if they were getting a sofa and she said there was no way to know for sure.

On another matter, I asked my agent if there was herbal tea on board the ship, and she said yes, there would be a wide variety of herbal teas including chamomile. In fact, the ship has no herbal tea except chamomile, and that is available only in the lounge or bar area for an extra charge. I didn't bring any tea with me. Last year, the opposite happened. I had asked before traveling, and the agent of that cruise line said there wasn't any herbal tea, so I brought a Ziploc container holding several dozen bags of tea. The ship had a variety of ten herbal teas offered in the buffet as well as the dining rooms.

The agents have a huge amount of information to keep track of, so knowing which ship has what characteristics is nearly impossible.

There are forums for individual cruise ships where you can join as a member and ask questions of travelers who were on that ship before. You can even ask about individual cabins.

Try www.cruisecritic.com and type in your ship's name. Do not rely on an individual's answer to your questions as they may be mistaken. I asked questions of several passengers who mentioned they were about to travel on the ship I was to take in a few months.

I asked if there were HDMI outlets on the TV and also if there was herbal tea. Both passengers shared incorrect information. I don't know why they missed the ten varieties of herbal teas. Missing the HDMI slot is understandable, as the ports are on the back of the TV. If you can't live without something, it's good to bring it with you.

Park a shopping bag in the corner of a room, and as you use or see things around the house that you won't need to use before the trip begins, put them in the bag. For example, the packable rain poncho you saw at the checkout counter at the dollar store might be a good addition. Doing a little at a time makes packing easier when you need to put it all together.

Start thinking about special clothing or shoes you might need to take. It might take time to find that perfect dress or break in a new pair of shoes.

Chapter Two: To-Do List before Leaving Home

Go through your credit card bill to see if there are monthly bills that can be put on vacation hold, like computer services, television or satellite contracts, newspapers, phones, etc. My post office only allows mail to be held for one month. Either have someone pick up your mail or pay for a service to hold your mail for you. Go through your check book to see what you normally pay monthly and arrange to have automatic payments made. If you already have automatic pay service, be sure you have enough money in your bank account to cover all your costs.

Keep in mind the charges you will have along the way while traveling as well as the automatic charges made by the cruise ship for on-board expenses, gratuities, and shore excursions. Review several months and list the average amount taken out of your bank each month; then add what you think you might spend for the four months.

Make a list of important phone numbers and passwords. It's easy to forget those numbers when you stop using passwords or stop calling a best friend for a few days or weeks. In case of emergencies, have all your family's numbers with you. Add the numbers of close friends. Take all your passwords. You never know when you may need to get into your bank account or cell phone account. You might read in the ship's newspaper that the stock market is expected to drop and you want to sell some stock. The password to the brokerage account might escape your memory since your last use of the site.

Let a neighbor know you will be gone for a long time in case something has changed with your house and give them emergency numbers to contact. A water leak for a month went unnoticed until finally a neighbor saw the pool of water in the yard and called a friend who hired someone to solve the problem. My water bill was over $500 (US) when I returned. When the lawn mowing didn't get done, a neighbor saw a yellow notice on my door warning the owner to cut the grass or the neighborhood association would fine the owner $300. The neighbor paid her gardener to mow the lawn for me.

Close all blinds in the house. Think about what temperature you want in the house while away or turn the thermostat off completely. Turn off your hot water tank. Turn off the water to the house at the main valve in case a water pipe breaks, a leak develops in an ice-making hose or the hose breaks leading to a washing machine.

Advise those who send regular incoming emails that you won't need them while away as they can become a hassle if your ship charges per use for downloading. I receive a lot of jokes, political news, ads from favorite stores and YouTube videos of music or photographs. Unsubscribe or tell friends to put you on hold for forwarded messages while you are away.

Your local library will have eBooks to download without charge, and each library works differently, so inquire. My library allows ten eBooks for check out at one time, and they become in-active and useless after three weeks. You can download them to any device like a computer, laptop, notebook, iPad, cell phone or Kindle. You have to have an Amazon.com account.

You can put books on hold and the library sends you an email when the book is available. I download ten books; in case I start a book and don't like it, I can move on to another. Keep a list of the books you have read with you or on your device so you don't check out books you've read before.

With more time for relaxing and reading, plan ahead. IF you have unlimited ship Wi-Fi, or you get to a port with Wi-Fi a few days before the three weeks is up, then go to Amazon.com and remove the finished books from your contents and devices section of your Amazon account. Then access the library web site and download more books to keep your maximum amount at ten. If you run out of books that you want to read before you reach the next port with Wi-Fi, then have alternate plans for passing time. You can always have a few dozen free Kindle books on your device at all times. Go to Amazon.com and type "free Kindle books" and thousands will come up in dozens of genres. Those books stay on your device for many months before they become in-active.

Taking paper books is something to consider for their weight and size. Ships have libraries, but finding your favorite author may or may not work.

My first cruise, the passengers were great about giving their books to the library for sharing after they read them. On a daily basis there might be 25 books to go through. My second cruise I heard passengers say they would rather share with a group of friends, and I have never seen one book on the sharing shelves. That library had no best-seller authors available to check out.

Unless your house will be occupied, think about food products in both pantry and refrigerator. Clean entire contents of refrigerator the day before you leave. So as to not encourage insects or rodents I put all food products like pasta, coffee, spices, staples like sugar and flour in a big Rubbermaid plastic container.

If you have any signs of insects, rodents or moths in your house, make plans to hire a pest removal service, or at the very least, spray inside everywhere so you don't return to a house full of roaches, mice or moths. Do research online to find out the latest advice for such protection.

Chapter Three: Documents for Trip

A few weeks before your departure, your ship will provide cruise documents to fill out and bring with you. You won't be allowed to board the ship without the documents.

The documents will be located on the cruise ship website under "Manage My Trip" or "Trip Personalizer", etc. or they will be mailed to you. Read the small print so you will understand what is provided and what is your responsibility.

Major items to complete, months before you leave, include the visas needed for each country you visit. To get started, you can hire visa agents online to do this for you for an additional cost, or your travel agent or the ship may recommend a particular company to help you with visas.

To save money, you can do the research yourself. Simply go to Google and type in "Does an American (or list your home country) citizen need a visa for Sri Lanka", for example. Look for a site that is an official site from that countries' government, not a private visa agent. Agents will charge you for their service.

Rules are different for every country and the type of visa needed will vary for every country. When comparing visas with other passengers I found that my Indian visa was good for ten years while a British citizen's Indian visa was good for one year and the same for China.

Many countries allow you to get an electronic visa online without charge or for very little cost. [Examples are Australia or Sri Lanka]. The company the ship recommends to help with visas may give you important free general information.

For example, there are different types of visas. For Sri Lanka, since you are staying less than 48 hours, you can apply for a transit visa which is free. You fill out the application online, and their government organization sends you an authorization you can then print and carry with you.

Australia does the same thing; however, they charge a small fee.

India offers a complicated visa and visa rules change all the time. For citizens of the US, the Indian visa offers an application that can be printed from the internet page.

Read all the rules carefully and send all the required documents to the embassy or consular office recommended on their site. Always use a FedEx envelope for return so it can be tracked in case it gets lost.

Allow plenty of time to get it but read the requirements for all visas to make sure they will be in effect while you are in that country. Some visas are only good for a certain time period or begin on a certain date.

Usually you have to provide proof of your travel plans, with a copy of airline and ship reservations. A Sri Lanka visa is good for only a few weeks starting the date of your arrival. Use caution with the correct dates.

If you are a British or Australian citizen, you may have to make a physical appearance at the embassy to get an Indian visa.

See information on Google and read others' experiences going through this procedure. It can be quite time consuming. Take extra care to check all documents required are with you.

The China visa rules changed after I got my very expensive Chinese visa for more than $200. They required an overnight FedEx round trip and a $150 visa fee. If you are taking a ship's shore excursion, find out if you still need a visa. If you are staying less than 48 hours in your arrival city, you may not need a visa for China, but these rules change and need to be verified for your particular time of travel.

Some countries offer an electronic visa if you are arriving into a listed airport, but this service doesn't apply for ships arriving at a seaport. Double check the latest rules as the rule for India just changed as I write today. Now passengers on cruise ships can get electronic visas the same as airline passengers for US citizens.

Rules are very confusing. Check the small print on the visa page. Many travel agents have not read the small print. Two years ago, there were 36 passengers who had to leave my ship in Dubai as they had the type of visa for airport arrival only.

They had to pay their own expenses for the next five days and fly into Sri Lanka, totally missing India. Some passengers said it cost more than $2000.

One entertainer had relied on her travel agent to get the correct visas and she missed her job on board the ship.

It is not the ship's responsibility to arrange or make sure you have all your proper documents. They will ask you to leave the ship if you don't have them in some cases.

On this year's cruise, some countries allowed the passengers to stay on board if they didn't have the proper visa, rather than being forced to disembark and fly to a later port.

Passports have to have at least six months of validity before expiring for all foreign travel.

In addition, there must be enough free space or blank pages for stamping visas. The larger countries don't stamp passports but scan them instead.

❧ Chapter Four: Luggage Choices

Well in advance of your trip, think about the type of luggage and what you want to limit yourself to take. If you are flying, your first bag might be free up to 50 lbs. Check the current status for your airline. There are a few foreign carriers that have weight limits of 44 lbs. and you pay for the first bag. The 2nd bag will be between $50 and $100 and you usually save money by paying online before you get to the airport. Carry-on luggage is different with American carriers and foreign so check all details. With an American carrier you might be allowed to carry-on one bag as a "roll-aboard" or medium duffel on wheels, [22"x15"x9"]. There are rules concerning a personal-sized back pack, computer bag or purse size to fit under your seat. Foreign carriers have different rules and usually limit carry-ons to one piece under 10K in weight. And unlike American carriers they will weigh your carry-on and put a carry-on tag on it.

I read before my first world cruise that some beds are only seven inches off the floor, and most luggage will not fit under your bed for storage while cruising. I found a totally collapsible bag that sits on six wheels and has sections to make it taller or shorter. I found it on www.ebay.com for $25 and it can stand as tall as five feet or zip down to two feet tall which is how I use it. When not in use I simply squish it down to a few inches and roll it under the bed. Suggestion: try www.cruisecritic.com to find your cruise ship and ask people if luggage can be stored under the beds. Also ask if that particular ship allows you to store your luggage elsewhere while not in use as some do and some do not. If your luggage fastens in the middle section (meaning the zipper runs around the middle instead of around the outer edge), then you can open it up to lay flat under the bed which doubles as a sort of extra drawer to store things that aren't used very often. In the house wares or closet/storage section of department stores like www.walmart.com, these wonderful packable drawers cost less than $5. They come folded in a tiny pouch and open to huge extra storage drawers for under the bed and are clear to easily find things. I put extra cosmetics, my first aid kit, extra protein bars, rain gear, etc. in Ziploc bags for under the bed storage until I need it.

If your carry-on is a "roll-aboard", make sure you find out if it will fit under your bed. Some people store their luggage in their closet but that takes up precious closet space you need for shoes and long pants and dresses to hang properly. I use a soft-sided, canvass type of duffel on wheels and pack anything I would not want to live without on the cruise, like a couple favorite outfits, favorite shoes, etc. For my personal carry-on, I have always used a backpack; it doubles its use and can be carried on shore excursions for purchases made, camera, water bottle, sunglasses, and hat. In that bag, which is very expandable, I pack things that I absolutely could not live without or would find hard to replace along the way like all electronic equipment, medications, first aid kit, vitamins, camera equipment, all money (see chapter on money) and jewelry. Always use luggage on wheels. Distances can be great in airports, and finding porters to carry your luggage for you is not always easy. I always make sure my carry-on has wheels as well. I set the backpack on top of the bigger carry-on piece and hold on to both pieces at once while moving around. In foreign airports, the remote gates can force long walks through duty-free areas. Walking to immigration and customs after arrival may seem like miles when you are carrying heavy bags in your arms. Most foreign airports have free luggage trolleys to use when you retrieve your checked baggage after you go through immigration. Credit cards were widely accepted at trolley rental places when checking in, where they charge a fee, usually around $5. Trolleys are never allowed past security check points, so keep that in mind if using one.

Chapter Five: Considerations for Packing

Preparation and Packing Tips

Think about the type of ship you are traveling on. A more expensive cruise means more formal nights and more formal wear in general. On an informal night, a woman can get by with more casual clothing, like capris or nice pants and tops on a more casual ship with dressy flip flops. A man can get by with a short-sleeved shirt on a more casual ship compared to the required jacket every night on a more formal, expensive ship.

I heard a man say on a sea day to another man, "Have you gone mad yet?" The friend replied, "Yes, you really can get bored on a world cruise!" Making sure you are prepared for long sea days is crucial to a smooth trip. Lying in a lounge chair is wonderfully relaxing if you are that type. If not, make sure you have books to read and projects to work on, or that you intend to get involved with ship activities like quizzes, games, lectures, craft, art, language, fitness or dance classes. Soaking in the steam or sauna is great for relaxing before bed time, and some ships have outdoor movie theaters for evening movies.

What to do in the evening if you are not a party person? There will be some sort of planned activity in the main theater every night but if you eat at the first seating and go to the first performance you may be free by 9:00 PM to go to piano bars, game shows, karaoke, etc. Sometimes the dancing doesn't start until 11:00 PM. Some ships offer a good selection of movies on room TV screens and others offer one movie choice per day. Most TVs have an HDMI slot in them, so if you have a laptop with you, it's possible to watch your own movies or videos you never have time to see, or to work on editing them on sea days. It can be fun to use your movies on flash drives for those evenings when you just want to chill in your room.

If you are cold-blooded or shiver easily, then exchange capris for long pants and short sleeves for long sleeves. I wear leggings or tights under pants, and I have silk, long underwear to wear under tops for chilly air-conditioned times. Pack clothing suited to your comfort level and the climate of your shore excursions. The main thing to keep in mind is flexibility with clothing. Take things that can work in different situations. If you never intend to sun on the beach, or swim and snorkel from the excursion boat, or use the ship's pool or jacuzzi, then forget the swim wear. The type of ship will suggest more or less formal clothing.-The culture of the people might influence the type of clothing. Americans are often casual and British may be more conservative. American women seldom wear dresses except for a formal evening. A week-long cruise out of Florida might call for cruise and beach wear, but no dresses except for one formal night.

Length of cruise will determine how many formal nights. Check your ship's "Manage My Trip" or "Trip Personalizer" feature for the climate at each port to help you decide what type of shore-excursion clothing to take. I got by with wearing the same type of clothing for excursions that I would wear around the ship on a sea day. Rough activities, like horseback riding or 4x4 jeep trips in the desert or rain, will require more thought. Consider other factors. Do you always eat in dining rooms or mostly in the more casual buffet or by the pool? What is your attitude about wearing the same clothing over and over? Are you the type that needs to have a different outfit every night? Yes, it is fun to dress up but the luggage and closet space the formal wear takes up is something to consider. Is the type of clothing you are bringing "dry clean only" or hand/machine washable? Read chapter on laundry.

To begin the packing, I empty a space in my closet just for the cruise trip. I've already made a list on paper of what I think I will need for the basics. I hang everything so I can see exactly the quantity and how well items match other items. All pants and tops are interchangeable with jackets, sweaters, scarves, and accessories. I am very conservative with the amount of clothing I take. Carrying extra luggage is not my idea of a vacation, and life is much simpler with fewer choices. A good rule of thumb is to pack for a two-week trip for clothing. Nobody will ever see you again, and nobody will be counting how often you wear a particular item.

I buy a box of the largest Ziploc bags I can find. These could be 2.5 gallons or larger. I roll my clothes and put as many as I can in one bag. I put all bras and panties in one bag and pajamas and socks in one bag. Squeeze all the air out of the bag before zipping closed. You will end up with cubes that pack on top of each other and the clothing stays close to wrinkle free. This protects your clothes from shifting around and ending up as one big mess when you open the bag. I wrap each pair of shoes in a separate plastic grocery-type bag and stuff them around the other cubes. All cosmetics, first aid, electronics, pens and notebooks go into individual bags as well. This keeps everything in order and protects them from getting bent or misplaced during travel. Buy packing cubes on www.ebay.com or www.amazon.com in different sizes.

Cold Weather

Weight depends on how cold you get. For the first few days of a cruise out of Europe in January, many wear a cashmere sweater, but sweaters take up a lot of space when packing. Air-conditioned areas on some ships are cold, so it is wise to be prepared. You can always remove something if dressed in layers. Wear your winter coat if traveling by air with a weight limit. World cruises will visit ports in colder climates, and many leave from Europe in January. A medium-weight coat can be worn in more places. Put a sweater or jacket underneath for winter places like Europe or northern China. Coats and jackets worn on planes are not counted in your carry-on weight limit.

Hats

Hats can be a problem to pack if delicate. Bring one to shade the face, like a straw or baseball type, and one with strap around neck for boat rides and windy days. On www.ebay.com, look for a folding baseball cap which conserves space for packing and carrying in backpack or purse. Columbia makes nylon-brimmed hats that are totally packable and have chin straps.

🦅 Chapter Six: For Women

Pants

I suggest basic colors to mix and match with contrasting tops for eight pair, all in blacks, white, or grey. Pack one pair of a jean type in blue, black, or grey to wear in colder weather or on rough shore excursions like 4x4s or horseback riding, two pair of dressy pants for nighttime wear, two pair of casual for daytime wear, two pair of capris or shorts for warm weather, and one pair for exercise room. I love www.chicos.com for their travelers' clothing as it never wrinkles and can be washed in the sink and dries in hours. I have a pair of black and a pair of tan for evening wear. Keep in mind how you will clean your clothing and how often. That will help determine how much to take. Anything with polyester, nylon, or rayon is less likely to wrinkle and easy to wash in a sink and hang to dry. I am very practical. All my clothing is hand washable except for formal wear. Most of my daytime wear is the brand "Columbia" which is nylon, no wrinkle, and hand washable. Linen and cashmere are fun to wear but harder to clean and keep fresh looking. Some ships have dry cleaning services, so those types of clothing can be dry-cleaned for an added expense. One cotton dress shirt was $7 for cleaning on the ship, so keep expenses in mind when bringing along "dry clean only" clothing, like formal wear or men's jackets/pants. Silk is a wonderful travel fabric, and most silk items are hand washable and look nice with careful ironing.

Tops

The twenty tops I suggest are broken down as follows. Five tops for evening wear with nice pants. They can be sheer tops worn over tanks, (which a lot of women wear), tunic length tops, sequined tanks, or anything considered dressy. Daytime wear are tops that go with your pants, capris or shorts for day use. Two tee shirts or short-sleeve blouses along with a mixture of another seven. Reel Legends makes nylon tops that wash in the sink and dry within hours. They are casual and easy to care for. About nine tops that can be worn for sea days and shore excursions. Sleeveless tops are great (if you don't tend to get chilly from air conditioning) or substitute additional long sleeves if you do get cold. I take a variety of fabrics and sleeve lengths depending on the weather outside and the coolness inside. For fun, I suggest some tops, about six, that might be considered cruise wear in whatever style you love. You will see women wearing sheer bat-wing tops over swim wear or over a tank top and also bright-colored fabrics, especially after visiting a tropical port. Tunic-length tops are popular for day or evening wear. Some of these tops could be worn in the evening with nice pants and a tank underneath on informal nights. All my tops are polyester or nylon, except for a couple of long-sleeve tops which are cotton blends and warmer. When the tops are rolled and put together in Ziploc bags, they become a small cube to pack. If you don't mind fewer choices, then take less. I'm very observant about what people wear, and I often see a woman wearing the same thing over and over. One woman on a tender told me, after I told her I loved her blouse, that she wore it every day. It was a loud pink and purple flowered button-down silk short sleeved shirt. She washed it every night and didn't care what people thought. She just felt comfortable in it and loved it so much.

Dresses and Formal Wear

Americans are more casual and don't wear dresses as much as European women do. On British ships the women wear dresses during the day and most evenings whether the dinnertime calls for casual or formal. Last year, I took five knee-length dresses and wore them all the time. However, this year, I trimmed down the weight and only took one casual dress and have worn it about once a week. Women wear long dresses at night, (the casual type with flowers/prints) as well as around the pool. Fabrics with nylon or polyester, wrinkle free, are best. Your cruise ship will inform you as to how many formal nights you'll have a few weeks before travel. Use that as a guide and think about whether you can wear the same dress again and again or are the type that needs something different. I had 26 formal nights on a British ship last year and took five, long, formal dresses and wore them all a few times each. This year, on a more casual ship, we have 17 formal nights, and I packed one black dress along with three glitzy, bling jackets and two shawls, so essentially, I have five formal outfits using one basic black long dress. The jackets are a red sequined, a silver rhinestone, and a black sheer with embroidery, {different enough that anyone seeing me would think I have a different dress on). On the casual ship this year, most women wear knee length dresses or cocktail dresses. Maybe 20% wear long evening-type gowns. However, I felt more comfortable in a long gown, since all the men were in jackets and some (10%) in tuxes.

Last year, a woman brought 26 formals for 26 formal nights. I brought five and decided that wearing a formal dress five times for two hours was not worth the extra weight and hassle. About 95% of the women wore long, elegant formal dresses. I took a wilder looking black, strapless dress made of satin with a peacock print around the bottom, and I felt out of place wearing it. The average age on world cruises is about 70. The gal wearing the five-inch stilettos gathered a lot of attention.

Pajamas

There is not much weight in these items, so the emphasis is on comfort and convenience. Every woman will have personal preferences that control her choices. One pair of lightweight pajamas washable in sink and not silk as it needs ironing. Robe only if needed around your room companion.

Bras and Panties

Four bras, including one strapless, if needed for formal dress. Be sure to choose bra colors that match your clothing, like darker colors for dark clothes, etc. Pack 7 pair of panties (and bring nude or white ones for white pants). I wash mine in the sink once a week, and most cruise ships have a line in the shower to hang clothing on to dry.

Socks and Leggings

This will depend on what type of shoes you bring and if you wear socks in the evening with flats and pants. Four pair of white crew socks if you bring tennis shoes. Two pair black warmer socks for cold weather and chilly evenings in the theater. Adjust for your type of shoes. Pant socks or knee-high socks made of thin nylon are easy to pack and wear with pants.

Leggings are great to wear with long tunic tops/dresses or tights/pantyhose to wear under pants in the evenings if it's cold in the dining room and theater.

Jackets and Sweaters

One jacket for daytime, (lightweight), and pack one jacket or sweater for nighttime. For daytime, pack a front opening type that goes with all your clothing. I take all grey, black or white pants and capris and contrasting colorful tops so the jacket is grey for daytime. At night, a sweater or jacket that is a simple solid color is perfect. For sweaters, I take a long tunic length 33" grey sweater that goes with everything. A long wide black wool shawl is perfect for any occasion. A tan or lighter color shawl to wear with the tropical patterned sheer tops works well.

Shoes

Conserve on space with less shoes. Most important will be a comfortable pair for port excursions with extensive walking in mind. I take tennis shoes that are well worn and are my most comfortable shoes. Also needed are a pair for daily wear on the ship, like sandals or flipflops. For evening wear, I bring two pair: one a little more formal. A flat pair of ballet type or a slip-on is good for pants and for rough sea nights. High heels are not worn much due to movement of the ship and age of the passengers.

Most women wear an open toe shoe with straps across the toes and a strap around the ankle. A small wedge heel or short heel, like 1 ½ inches, or less is most popular. Never take new shoes that are not broken in. People do not look at your feet and won't care if you don't have brown shoes to go with the tan pants.

Some of the more expensive ships will be very rigid about footwear; they may object to sandals that look like flipflops, despite how fancy they are. If the strap comes up between the first and second toe and has an open back you might be asked to change shoes. However, I wear that kind of shoe on a less formal cruise, and I have never been asked to change.

Flip flops are great for public areas where there is water, such as the steam room, saunas, pools, and Jacuzzis where they protect against germs. Water shoes are also great for swimming where the bottom is uncertain, like around sharp, rocky ocean floors or tubing excursions in rivers. If you have time, you can order cheap ones on www.ebay.com from China for a few dollars but check their size chart as the shoes are sold in Asian sizes and may be too small when they arrive.

Fun-To-Wear Cruise Clothing

Include some fun clothing; after all, you are on a cruise. On sea days, many women wear knee-length sundresses or beach-type cover-ups over bathing suits. Sleeveless and just-below-the-knee in wild designs like a tie-dyed or batiked fabric are the most popular. Along the way, people buy clothing made locally, like wide legged Asian elephant pants or long Indian saris or wild tropical sheer poncho tops from South Pacific islands.

 Chapter Seven: For Men

Shoes

One pair for long walking excursions that are comfortable and broken in. One pair for daily sea days like tennis, deck, flip flops, or slip-ons. Two pair for night wear with one being more formal, like a slip-on or tie-dress shoe.   A shoe like a Rockford tie shoe could be worn for almost everything, meaning a man could get by with two pairs of shoes for the entire trip. Some fitness gyms won't allow any shoes except rubber-soled or tennis types of shoes. On a more casual ship, open-toed shoes are acceptable, like a Teva sandal with toe and ankle straps in the dining room on an informal night. I've been on many ships that require closed-toed shoes for men in the dining room for meals. To be very conservative only two pairs are needed: one tie career/business-suit style and one more casual for every day, gym, or around the pool.

Suits, Jackets, or a Tuxedo

Only one tux is needed. Men can wash the white shirt as often as desired. One dark suit can take the place of the tux. Some ships are very formal, and most men wear a tuxedo on formal nights. To save space, bring only two sport coats or suit jackets, one in a light color and one in a dark color. Some ships require a jacket every night so use your own judgment as to how bored you might get with your jackets. A change in shirt color and/or a tie helps to create variety. One sweater for cool nights that is a little more formal, like a solid color to go with all pants. One lightweight jacket for chilly days or air conditioning turned up high. Cruise ships can be very cold and very warm so pack clothing to adjust to both. Layering is the best answer. One lightweight winter coat for excursion days. Check climate in each city or check your ship's web site for the average temperatures for shore excursions.

Pants, Capris, Shorts

Three pants for a basic wardrobe for evening in cotton or polyester mix or polyester. Four pair for daytime wear (two pair of long and two shorter pairs like capris or shorts).

Shirts

Four long sleeve shirts for evening wear, one being white for formal night or a tuxedo shirt. Four short/long sleeved for daytime sea days or shore excursions. One short sleeve for fitness center or gym.

Socks and Underwear

Seven pairs of socks to wash once a week: white crew-style for tennis shoes, or black or tan to match clothing. Seven underwear pairs to wash only once a week. Cotton dries in a day, but nylon or polyester will dry faster. Microfiber briefs are hard to find except on travel clothing sites listed below. Nylon boxers are easy to find at cheap discount houses. Nylon briefs are available sometimes at the cheaper stores like www.walmart.com but don't count on it. They keep you from having to have your underwear hanging for 24 hours in the shower to dry.

Pajamas and Robe

One pair of pajamas and no robe unless one is necessary because of a travel companion.

Swim Suit and Tee Shirts

A swim suit which could be used for gym. Men buy tee shirts from various local ports. Words like Barbados, Petra, begin to appear on dozens of tee shirts. Bring a couple if you wish.

 Chapter Eight: Jewelry

Don't bring any of your favorite jewelry, as it might get stolen or lost. Try to mix and match jewelry to go with several outfits. Six or less necklaces, a few pairs of earrings and a couple of different costume-type rings might be adequate. A silver chain is good to wear with a variety of pendants. Glitzy, bling, or fake diamonds are fun for formal wear.

Be cautious about wearing silver or gold into hot tubs, pools, or the ocean. The metals can be damaged. Keep all jewelry in the cabin's safe unless wearing it. When you go ashore for snorkeling trips, remove all your jewelry for safe keeping. At some ports, thieves gather around tourist sites. Leave your expensive watches and jewelry in the cabin safe.

Chapter Nine: Cosmetics

I take everything out of its original container to save space. I put everything in Ziploc bags. The bag gets smaller as you use the products, so you come back with smaller containers. I put liquids in small bottles like an empty prescription or aspirin type of bottle. Don't forget to label the container with permanent marker. Wrap clear tape over the marked label as it might rub off, and you'll not know if the bottle is shampoo or sunscreen. Test the bottle when filled before packing. Double wrap all liquids in two bags in case the pressure from the flight causes the bottle to spring a leak. I have opened my bag to find shampoo or body oil oozing all over the inside of its double layer plastic. A formal dress would be ruined if covered in body oil!

To get an idea of how much you use of something, start a few months before the trip and measure how much toothpaste, for example, you use in a two-month period. Two 5 oz tubes of toothpaste will just about be enough for the entire trip, if brushing twice a day. A 44 oz. package of dental floss is not quite enough. If you washed your hair every five days, then put 24 squirts of shampoo in a vitamin bottle about 3 inches tall. Saves so much space. Go through your cosmetics and make a list of all the little things you can't live without for four months, like a nail file, nail clippers, tweezers, nail polish, nail polish remover, Chapstick, make-up, shampoo, conditioner, body lotion, comb, brush, clips for hair, rubber bands for hair, deodorant, razor plus battery style for intimate spots, sunscreen. Some ships provide free shampoo, conditioner, and body lotion but some only for suites. A small battery-operated razor is perfect for bikini trimming. It can be found in discount stores in the cosmetic department and is designed for trimming noses, ears, and facial hair.

🎁 Chapter Ten: Money

Money issues are frustrating, if not figured out in advance of travel. Credit cards are the safest way to deal with large sums for shore excursions or purchases abroad, if not using ship's excursions. Some large-city taxis even take credit cards.

Prepare for added surcharges for using cards everywhere. Many credit cards charge both a currency conversion fee and also a charge for foreign transactions.

Not all cards will work all the time. A friend just told me they wanted to take the optional helicopter trip over the Great Barrier Reef. It was quite expensive, and everyone around him wanted to pay with a charge card. The machine the operator used would only accept certain cards, and he was one of the lucky ones that was able to take the trip.

I've been in stores where my card was not accepted but yet the person behind me had the same type of Visa card and theirs was.

Many places do not take debit cards or honor companies like American Express. Taking two cards allows you to have an extra card if one doesn't work but could be riskier to lose or have stolen.

Take a photo with your cell phone of your cards, both front and back, in case they are stolen or you lose them so you will have the collect phone number to call to report them missing with the correct card number.

Printing front and back views on a sheet from your home computer printer is another way to have a record of the card information. Do not do this in a drugstore or discount store as those machines may store the information and then print it. I was told by the store manager that information is kept for a long time before it is deleted.

Your cruise ship will take out payments for your shore excursions, gratuities and on-board charges every few weeks.

Last year I paid for Wi-Fi for the entire cruise and they mistakenly charged me for the entire $1000 charge again, two weeks later. It took several weeks to clear up the mistake but in the meantime my charge card was charging me a 22% interest payment as I had set up for the card to only make the minimum amount of monthly payment needed automatically.

How much cash to take is a question that has no answer. Rooms have safes to keep valuables in, like money, cards and jewelry, so more is probably better than not enough.

However, just about every city has an ATM machine which gives you cash in the local currency. You can get local currency on board your ship but not against your account. You have to change cash for cash, and some ships only take the currency of their home country, which in my two experiences were British pounds.

In my two world cruises I have never used an American hundred-dollar bill which one might think is the most logical to take.

More than half the countries I have visited in the past take American dollars for everything. The American one-dollar bill is used most frequently, and I would suggest taking two hundred dollars in one-dollar bills. Smaller cities or islands I found on the last cruise would not take one-dollar bills as store owners said the banks were tired of so much paper money. Having a little of all small denominations is more practical. I like to take cash compared to using an ATM machine. My suggestion is something like two hundred dollars in ones, and a hundred each in fives, tens and twenties. The rest I carry in one hundred-dollar bills. This is totally a personal decision as to how to carry money in cash or get it along the way with an ATM.

Don't ever expect change in American dollars, however, which is why you want smaller bills. If something costs $11 and you offer a $20 bill, then you will get change in the local currency for the $9 value.

Small, independent tour operators will mostly take American dollars for tours. They won't have change in dollars so $20 bills are good for that situation.

Very important to remember when getting cash for a trip is to ask for brand new bills. A bank will always take time to find the newest bills they have or you can request brand new bills to pick up the next day.

The smaller the foreign city the pickier they are about this, and they won't take bills with any kind of bend in the corner or markings of any kind, including dirty, unclean old bills.

Remote areas, which probably won't be an issue on a cruise ship excursion, sometimes don't take certain denominations.

They have been warned by their governments of counterfeit currency in that amount at certain times. I was in Ethiopia once, and they would not take twenty-dollar bills for anything. That was all I had left and the hotel had to give me the room free, as there was nothing either of us could do.

Chapter Eleven: Purses and Tote Bags

Consider the following:
Small cross-over or messenger bag to carry cruise card to dining and theater at night.

Grocery sized bag for daytime to carry things needed for note-taking in classes, or towel, sunscreen, book or Kindle, and hat for lounging on deck.

Bring the backpack you used for carry-on while flying or a smaller packable, expandable backpack for shore excursions to carry swim wear, towels, water shoes, sunglasses, bottled water, sunscreen, jackets, rain gear, laptop or cell phone for shoreside Wi-Fi connections.

Don't overlook hats. Bring one to shade the face, like a straw or baseball type, and one with strap around neck for boat rides and windy days. On www.ebay.com, look for a folding baseball cap which conserves space for packing and carrying in backpack or purse. Columbia makes nylon-brimmed hats that are totally packable and have chin straps.

Chapter Twelve: First Aid and Medicines

You can buy almost anything abroad on port days, but expect to pay several times your cost at home. Plus, you won't have the item when you need it. A tiny bottle of hair conditioner or small tube of toothpaste was $17 In Panama. If you have favorite brands, buy enough for the trip. A good way to test how much you need is measure how much you use in a month, and take that times four.

Don't forget sea bands, various motion sickness tablets, anti-itch creams, safety pins, tiny sewing kit, 3 Band-Aids, ear plugs, Ciprofloxacin for diarrhea, Amoxicillin for bacterial cough, stool softener, laxative, Extra Strength Tylenol 500 mg., 50 tablets, ibuprophen, 50 tablets, Loratadine for itching, runny nose, and itchy eyes, cold day and night tablets, Benadryl or antihistamine for allergies/itching, Loperamide for diarrhea, vitamins.

I count out vitamins or supplements and put into Ziploc bags and, with a permanent marker, I label each bag as to what is in it and how often to take. The same idea works with all medications like Tylenol. As you use the products, the bag gets smaller. Prescription drugs take a little extra care for extended trips and most will require a doctor's okay for more than a 90-day supply. Take photos of all prescriptions before getting them filled in case you run out and need to get more along the way. In many countries, you only need to walk into a pharmacy and show them what you need and they will fill it. Sometimes, you will have to consult a clinic or doctor and simply have them write a new prescription if you run out. The medical department on ships is quite expensive for antibiotics, cough and cold medications, or any other drug, so try to bring your own. Since the doctors on board don't have your background medical records they tend to run lots of tests which can run into the thousands of dollars. Unless it's an emergency, most travel insurance plans won't pay for that type of bill.

Motion sickness is a worry for many, so come prepared. A doctor will give a prescription for a medication that goes directly into your blood and is patch worn, usually behind the ear. Read all about this type of drug as it can have some uncomfortable side effects when you stop taking it. Most motion sickness tablets are simply mild sedatives and make you sleepy. There are a few non-drowsy brands, and you will find more natural products like those made of ginger. Ginger ale, ginger snap cookies, ginger candy, crackers, and toast all help with motion sickness. Don't wait until you are sick to take any kind of medication as it works better to take before you get sick. Ships may provide a free tablet on rough sea days. But it will be a typical Dramamine tablet that will make you very sleepy.

Chapter Thirteen: Electronics

Think about what kind of electronics you want to take and all the attachments or equipment those items need, like special cords, plugs, or batteries. Months before the trip, make a list of the equipment you are taking, just to make sure you have enough batteries and spare charging cords. Battery-operated travel alarm clocks, shavers, toothbrushes, or cameras may need extra batteries. If you take items that use memory cards or micro SD cards, don't forget an adapter to transfer them onto a laptop or notebook, etc.

Flash USB drives are a must, if you do any type of sharing information with others, want the reception desk to print a document you have on your laptop or notebook, or for storing photographs to get them off of your memory or SD card. Bring extra ones, as you might lose one or forget the passengers name who was going to share his photos with you on your flash drive.

While standing in line, or as the English say in queues, a great way to pass the time is reading something on your tablet or Kindle. Waiting for a show to begin or a gangplank to open in order to disembark is boring and frustrating. The diversion of a good book helps pass the time.

One ship I was on had a single plug in the room. For two people, both charging computers, cell phones, notebooks, or Kindles, much was demanded from that one plug. Research online which adapter you will need for the home country of your ship. Next plug in an extension cord (check if you need the three-hole grounding type), then a plug that has three outlets. If you need more than three outlets, then plug in another three-way plug or extension cord. Bring a multi USB adapter if several devices need a USB charging port. Two sets of headphones are essential for listening to music in public places, on long, boring trips like a flight, or while jogging away those extra pounds from too many desserts.

If you are traveling to other countries before or after your long cruise, then research what type of electrical adapter you will need.

If you want to use the TV as a monitor, then you'll need an HDMI cord and possibly an audio cord. I have a tiny blue-tooth speaker that worked when I plugged in my notebook and turned on my music. On a different cruise, the only way it worked was with an audio cord (earphone jack) plugged into the TV to increase volume from my own personal movies.

Chapter Fourteen: Laundry, Storage, & Bathroom

Laundry

Formal wear is only worn for a few hours at a time. Last year's cruise had 26 formal nights, and this year there were 19. A man could bring four jackets and get by without dry cleaning them. Or he could wear the same tuxedo and only clean the white shirt every so often. Once a week I wash all lingerie in the room sink, and once every two weeks, I get by with washing everything else in the sink.

Every individual will have a method of cleaning clothing, so try to consider how much time you want to spend on hand or machine washing/drying versus bringing additional clothing. Check with your cruise line to see if they have washers, dryers, and irons for public use. Some offer free machines and others charge $2 for tokens to use, paid with your ship card. Test the iron before using as I used an untested iron on my white pants and quickly stopped due to the black marks the iron was making. It did wash out but what a time-consuming project. Laundry soap is about $2 per load. Bring a bottle of liquid soap or a Ziploc of powered if you want to save money. I use the bar or liquid soap in the cabin for my hand washing.

Storage

You may find ample storage in your cabin based on an inside twin and use of spaces under the beds. But some cabins are quite small.

If you pack using this book as a guide, you will have a few empty drawers to spare. The last ship had 24 drawers and a closet about six feet wide, with about ten permanent hangers in it. The inside twin rooms were 188 square feet. Most people leave behind any hangers they brought with them so you may be lucky when you ask your steward for extra hangers. I suggest going to a dry cleaner and getting some free wire hangers. Count the number of items you need to hang and bring that many with you. Tie them together with twist ties, or cable ties so they don't get bent in luggage.

Bring either safety pins or clothes pins to attach pants for hanging. Clothes pins will double for hanging wet clothing on the line in the shower as well. When organizing your room's drawers, keep clothing items near the closet or dressing area. In the drawers next to your bed, keep items you might need during the day or night like journals, books, maps, paperwork for shore excursions, etc. I use a bottom drawer for dirty clothes as it's easier to open and close rather than a plastic bag. Dirty clothes can get smelly so don't leave them in the open on a shelf or on the floor of the closet. Unless you have a balcony, there will be no fresh air.

Bathroom

Bathrooms are quite adequate on cruise ships. Some showers are smaller than others. The storage area is about six small shelves, usually hidden behind the mirrors. Keep all tiny loose objects in one of your packable cubes, a Ziploc bag or a soft cosmetic bag. There may be a hanging line high in the shower for drying hand-washed clothing. However, I have walked by other rooms, and clothing is hung on picture frames, mirrors and other objects that were not meant for that purpose. Most ships have the same environment ideas, like hanging your towels back up if you feel you can use them again. If not, put them on the tile floor. Some ships provide shampoo, conditioner, and hand lotion. Others offer them only for suite guests. To be safe, bring your own favorites in small containers. Measure how much you use in a one-week period and multiply that by the number of weeks you'll be gone. I can get shampoo for the entire trip into a 100 count Tylenol bottle. Turn the bottle upside down after filling to test it for leakage.

Chapter Fifteen: Security and Miscellaneous

Ship Security

The ship will x-ray your luggage after you hand it over for check in. There are items some ships won't allow which usually involves safety and liquor. Check the rules of the cruise line to find out what you can and cannot bring aboard in the way of liquor and wine. I'm guessing that dangerous items like knives and guns would be prohibited. My last cruise had both a quilting class and a knitters group, so I could assume that scissors were permitted. Each time you return from a shore excursion, your pack or bag will be x-rayed so don't do anything silly or stupid like sneaking drugs on board. Check with your individual ship on the rules for bringing liquor or wine from shore ports. In addition, expect dogs to be used not only for drug discoveries but for contraband food that might violate the legal protection to prevent fruit flies or contamination for the food industry in a country.

Most foreign countries require no food products brought into the country. Your ship will make an announcement before passengers disembark to a shore excursion. If you plan to pack a lunch, sneak an apple or fill a bag with nuts and cheese, forget it. If a dog used for finding food catches you, there might be a huge penalty to pay.

Business Cards

Business cards are a cheap and easy way to share your personal information with new friends or new potential business acquaintances you meet while traveling.

If you don't have any business or friendship cards, there are cheap sites where you can order hundreds printed very quickly. They allow you to design your own card, use one of their templates, or simply put your name, address, phone and/or email address on them.

Protecting your Things

You can use packable small bags for miscellaneous items, and Ziplocs work great.

Cable ties are great for locking items in place, like your luggage before traveling. If TSA gets in your bag, then the tie will be broken, and you will know the bag was opened, so double check all your belongings.

If you stay at a hotel the day before or after your cruise, then cable tie the luggage or put a small lock on it to keep curious hands out. It won't keep someone from stealing from your bag of course, as they can cut the tie off. But they would have to have a knife or scissors or nail clippers to do that, and it will keep those wanting a quick look from trying, unless they take the whole bag.

If you use a cable tie, keep a nail clipper in your shoulder bag or purse to cut the bag open when you need to get into it.

Years ago, nail clippers were not allowed in carry-on bags so I had to go to reception to borrow a scissors to open my bags.

Packable rain ponchos, like from the dollar store or discount house, are handy to keep in a pocket. Umbrellas are not necessary if you are trying to conserve space and you are taking the poncho.

Ziploc bags: take ½ dozen out of the box and roll them up with a rubber band. Great for carrying wet bathing suits or fruit or cookies back to room for a midnight snack. A 2.5-

gallon size or greater is perfect for storing dirty clothes or separating lingerie, etc. when packing.

Other Ideas

Magnets for metal cabin walls can help you keep track of itinerary, daily to-dos, or reminders. Pack pens, markers, notebooks for note taking, a diary or journal.

A lanyard for your cruise card; for women it's nice to just put the cruise card on a lanyard rather than carry a purse or tote all day, unless you have a pocket. Every time you leave the room, you will need it to get back into your room. If you check sites like ebay.com you will find 1000s of lanyards from China, beaded or woven in a rainbow of colors.

I bought a chain type for $.33 and most people think it's silver. Even the agent running the scanner when you get off the ship told me he loved it. Buy several to match clothing, as your card will be your lifeline to your room. It is your ID for any charges you make on the ship and your proof of being a ship's passenger when embarking and disembarking the ship. A good project I have heard many people bring, including myself, is sorting through hundreds of photographs if they are digital or on DVD's, etc.

Clips for back of chair to hold beach towel; it's available at dollar stores. Clothespins for hanging pants in closet, or use safety pins to save space when packing. Safety pins for tears in clothing or shoes.

Hangers

Wire clothes hangers from dry cleaners (free). Ships will supply around ten hangers per person so count how many extra to take. Or ask your steward the first day as most people leave their hangers on board when they leave and the steward will have extras sometimes.

Weight Control

The one thing nobody wants to leave the ship with is extra weight. And all the food choices make it hard to keep that from happening. There are decks for walking and a fitness center for more serious workouts and if one is not careful they might be one of the statistics for gaining a pound a week. It is a vacation and taking an hour a day to keep weight down feels like hard work. Put your favorite songs on your cell phone and listen to music while you work out.

My secret for keeping track of my weight is not a scale but a tape measure. Scales don't work well over water for some reason I don't understand. You might gain weight in your stomach but lose it in your muscles, but the scales tell you your weight is the same. If you measure and record around your middle section, always in the same place, like over your belly-button and again a few inches below that area, then you will see the changes in your weight on the tape measure. Bring the cloth type that rolls up into a tiny little ball.

Planning and Reminders

Blank calendar (or print blank calendar pages from free online sites) to put on the wall with a magnet. Write reminders of special events or shore excursions with a bold marker.

Living on a ship takes on a new lifestyle and it's not long before you develop a relaxed routine and begin to not even notice what day of the month it is. Mini daily newspapers are offered in several languages, but, without those, the days all seem to roll into everyday being just a new day not a certain day of the week.

Food and Special Diets

All special diets require letting your cruise company know your requirements several weeks before departure. Cruise companies are quite used to dealing with special diets if they can prepare lists in advance for what they need to buy. Sometimes it takes a little time to figure out what you can eat on a ship, as chefs might be used to serving food with more spices than you like, for example. Be patient in working with chefs onboard as they only want to please and will go out of their way to do so. The Executive Chef on my last cruise told me a woman only wanted unsweetened coconut milk to drink. However, in her pre-cruise request she only stated coconut milk. He showed her unsweetened almond, rice and soy milk but she was still not happy. I'm a vegan and it took about a week for the chefs to understand that I didn't like all the curry dishes nor the spicy food they were serving. With all the choices I am given, now I feel like I am in food heaven.

The Executive Chef, during the first week, told the vegans to be patient as our food is prepared as we order it, not earlier in the day, and we may have to wait a little longer than other passengers to get served. If I have a show I want to go to and getting a dessert might interfere with that timing, I mention it to my waiter and he makes sure I am served quickly. The crew members only want to please and will go the extra mile to help out.

If you require special foods that you assume will not be on the ship, then try to figure out a way to bring that along. For extra protein, I bring a jar of almond butter, as there are always good breads to spread it on. Sacks of nuts, protein bars, and protein powder (which I add to oatmeal in the mornings) assures me that I am getting enough protein. Your cruise ship's agent should know if your room will have a refrigerator. Mine said there was not one, but I could request a room with one if needed for medication, I found a good-sized one in my cabin. A refrigerator is great for little snacks you might carry back from a shore excursion or fruit leftover from breakfast for a morning snack or to keep a bottle of water cold. If you absolutely need a place for medication, then request a refrigerator when you make your booking.

Be patient with your waiters as many are new on the job and want to learn quickly how to deal with unusual situations like special diets.

Port Days: Research your Options in Advance

From the comfort of your home computer, you can dream and plan for port days and save a lot of frustration that comes from failing to plan for clothes and tools and even printouts that confirm your arrangements. For my first world cruise, I spent over two weeks researching every port for unusual excursions or to save money versus using the ship's excursions. The second world cruise I did very little research thinking I would take a "Hop on Hop off" bus or find a local tour operator. I don't feel like I missed much by doing the latter except, in a couple of ports, I heard other passengers talk about their great ideas that they found using independent tour operators. Either way you need to think about the type of excursion you take in order to plan clothing for that adventure.

Chapter Sixteen: Sites to Save Money and Time

www.chinavisa.com Residents of each country will have different procedures to apply for a China visa; at one point, for US citizens, it was not possible to get a Chinese visa unless applied for in person. Consider hiring a private visa company like the one in referred to above to do it for you. This company in my case was efficient, had reasonable charges, and went over my application before sending it to make sure all the forms are correctly filled in. There were some unusual questions they helped me with.

www.ebay.com has bargains, including new products and used clothing and shoes, cameras, underwater cameras and even tiny things like extra cords for cell phones and notebooks, adapters, special batteries, etc.

www.chicos.com for clothing for travelers with their Travelers Collection

www.beallsflorida.com for nylon clothing for travel like Columbia and Reel Legends for men/women

www.zappos.com for shoes that can be returned FREE if they don't fit or are uncomfortable

www.indianvisaonline.gov.in/evisa/Registration
   For Indian visa

www.travelnomads.com for travel insurance

www.cruisecritic.com for information about cruising on your particular ship and it's a way to talk to other cruisers

www.exofficio.com for travel clothing for sun protection and wrinkle-free clothing that is more sport and adventure wear

www.sportif.com for travel clothing for sun protection and wrinkle free features

www.rei.com for travel clothing for sun protection and wrinkle free features

www.vistaprint.com for inexpensive and fast business cards to share with new friends on your cruise

www.vacationstogo.com a great travel site for finding good deals on travel

www.tripadvisor.com the best site for reading reviews from other travelers on anything that has to do with travel

Author Page

Jackie Chase writes travel books and has garnered several dozen awards in international author competitions. Her first two books on cruising were about the world's largest cruise ship.

One of the themes in these books was the fascinating cultural blending of the ship's crew representing 79 nations. They worked closely together in friendship and respect to please the guests of the cruise line.

One book offered the cruising public a glimpse of the personalities of the crew, their countries, and their responsibilities aboard, all told with humor and nearly 100 photos behind the scenes of this floating resort.

The other book has become a morale-building tool for crewmembers, both new and veteran, as the crew's words offered practical ideas on how to build respect and teamwork out of a multi-cultural challenge to please the guest. The interior content of each was similar but the remainder catered to the crew or guests with additional information.

The author has cruised a number of times in the ships listed below with Royal Caribbean, Norwegian, Cunard, Carnival, P & O (around the world) and CMV (on the inaugural world cruise for the MV/Columbus).

Her other books:

See: www.JackieChase.com; www.WorldTravelDiva.com and www.CulturesOfTheWorld.com. Jackie has traveled to over 100 countries and specializes in staying in remote villages in order to use her keen observations and photo-journalism skills to share her insights with her reader fans.

She has traveled alone, with a child, with family, and with friends; she has earned over 32 awards from international book contests from 2014 to date of printing; she shares with the public many of the travel secrets she has experienced in her book titled,

"How to Become an Escape Artist" A Traveler's Handbook.

The Handbook was tested for several years with students in a college evening class, and they soaked up Jackie's hints and the many ways to avoid disappointment, reduce expenses and frustrations, navigate the issues of visas, language, customs, currencies, accommodations, transportation, attitudes, danger, travel alone, and other problems all covered in over 190 segments in the book. It is up to date with nearly 100 click links to hard-to-find websites dealing with all aspects of travel, including finding companions.

Her *"All Hands Working Together" Cruise for a Week: Meet 79 Cultures* book treats cruising in a unique way so cruise guests can learn about cultures and fascinating cruise ship operations; the reader experiences personal contact with crewmembers from many of the 79 countries they represent, and from many skills they possess.

An employee motivational book, *'24-7' Multi-Cultural Workers Find Diversity Recipe to Heal a Troubled World* is based on "All Hands" and also peeks behind the scenes of the world's largest floating resort to see how 79 different cultures work and live together '24-7'. Universally relevant stories created an inclusion recipe that celebrates human differences including race, customs, gender, age, religion etc. They open minds to cross-cultural awareness or respect in organizations worldwide. Current technology makes it possible to deliver an eBook to every worker in an organization to enhance its mission and stimulate a widely-shared attitude adjustment that produces success through cooperative creativity. Diversity at work pays creativity dividends for employer and worker. Imagine applying this team-building magic in government, campus, non-profit or business settings!

Jackie Chase has written definitive books on "People to Meet" in contrast to "Places to See". She convinces her readership to look beyond mountains, lakes and buildings to see world inhabitants of all continents as potential friends and shows how much we have in common. Her images tell stories and fascinate her fans. Another theme is the concern by thoughtful leaders about the vanishing cultures and traditional villages on every continent. They are simply overwhelmed by our electronic world, well-meaning schooling requirements and worldly exposure for children, and the ease with which tourists can interact and reach these remote villages. Jackie's images and commentary preserve for all time the stories of some of these traditional cultures.

She shows how to bridge gaps created by custom and language in *"100 People to Meet before You Die: Travel to Exotic Places"*. This book, [as well as the others], are available in color, grayscale, and, with stunning images in eBooks that come to life on backlit screens. This anthology involves 12 countries and contains 321 of those story-telling images and ward-winning prose about her adventures. For her fans of a particular country, she has twelve "singles" in print and in eBook format, plus at least one (Panama) translated into Spanish.

For children, from small up through teens, a "winner" of a book is ***"Giraffe-Neck Girl" Make Friends with Different Cultures***. It is about a ten-year-old girl in Thailand who warms the hearts of young and old as she shares her different life and customs.

Jackie Chase's 2016 book, ***"Walking to Woot" A Photographic Narrative Discovering New Dimensions for Parent-Teen Bonding*** has won 17 international awards in the genres of Parenting, Young Adult Non-fiction, Multi-Cultural, Cover Design, and Travel. It contains both poetic descriptions and visual ones with its nearly 170 images of life with stone-age tribal warriors who haven't changed customs in a thousand years. The New Guinea unclothed villagers welcomed Jackie and her blond 14-year-old daughter to pig roasts, unusual customs, and dances. Jackie Chase loves to hear from her fans and to see copies of reviews they submit to the web. Contact her at:
JakartaMoon@hotmail.com

BOOKS BY JACKIE CHASE: 2014/17
How to Become an Escape Artist: A Traveler's Handbook: (2014);
Giraffe-Neck Girl: Make Friends with a Different Culture (2014;)
100 People to Meet before You Die: Travel to Exotic Cultures (2014-6); "All Hands Working Together" Cruise for a Week: Meet 79 Cultures 2014); '24-7' Multi-Cultural Workers Find Diversity Recipe to Heal a Troubled World (2017)

AWARDS (15) FOR THE BOOKS LISTED ABOVE

Royal Palm Literary Award; National Indie Excellence Book Award; FAPA President's Book Award; Readers' Favorite Book Award; International Book Award; USA Best Book Award; Beverly Hills Book Awards

AWARDS (17) for: "Walking to Woot" A Photographic Narrative Discovering New Dimensions for Parent-Teen Bonding:

Beach Book-; & San Francisco-: Festivals; Beverly Hills Book Award in 3 Genres; Eric Hoffer Grand Prize Award in 2 Genres; Florida Authors and Publishers Association (FAPA, including cover award); International Book Award, Montaigne Medals; National Indie Excellence Award; Next Generation Indie Book Award in 2 Genres; Paris Book: Festival; Reader's Favorite Award in 3 Genres.

BUSINESS BOOK BY JACKIE CHASE: 2017

'24-7' Multi-Cultural Workers Find Diversity Recipe to Heal a troubled World: See above description [Sharing inclusion/diversity ideas with employees/students/managers in businesses, charities and governments using inexpensive eBook distribution methods to reach every participant in the organization].

All books are available at: www.AdventureTravelPress.com and www.inclusionPLUSdiversity.com

Jackie Chase

No stranger to travel, this photo-journalist has lived among many cultures to observe daily life in 100+ countries. Garnering over 32 competition awards for her 5 major books, she observes and shares stories about the lives of remote villagers and fascinating cultures. Here, the "villagers" share a ship while discovering secrets to harmonious ways cultures can live and work together. Please help her spread these stories of respect and inclusion by sharing this book with your friends and family.

E-book: ISBN-978-1-937630-24-9

Print-Grayscale: ISBN-978-1-937630-23-2

www.AdventureTravelPress.com

Made in the USA
Las Vegas, NV
10 May 2021